Thus Saith The Lord

Prophecy & Tongues

Verse by Verse through 1 Corinthians 14

David Chapman

Thus Saith The Lord
Prophecy & Tongues
Verse by Verse through 1 Corinthians 14

David Chapman

All Bible quotations are from the New King James Version unless
otherwise noted.

TRU Publishing
P.O. Box 201
Thatcher, Arizona 85552

Table of Contents

Introduction

As a pastor for over 20 years, I have seen regular occurrences of the power of the Holy Spirit in manifestation. What an awesome privilege we have as believers. I have also witnessed an enormous amount of confusion and ignorance on the subject of the gifts of the Holy Spirit. Much of the lack of understanding is directed at the vocal gifts – prophecy, tongues and interpretation of tongues.

In the 14th chapter of 1 Corinthians, Paul sets forth very clear instructions on the use of these vocal gifts in the assembly. In this book, I will go verse by verse through the entire chapter in order to provide enlightenment on this subject.

If you have questions that are not answered in this book, please feel free to email me at TheRiverAZ@gmail.com.

David Chapman

Background

Corinth was a great city. Politically, it was the capital city of the Roman province of Achaia, a territory including nearly all of Greece. Corinth was a great commercial center. Nearly half a million people lived there.

The apostle Paul had spent 18 months founding the church at Corinth. He was their spiritual father (1 Corinthians 4:15). When he left, he left He left Priscilla and Aquila, fellow apostles, there to continue the work (Acts 18:18-22). While in Ephesus, Paul received unfavorable reports about the Corinthian church which prompted him to write his first letter to this church, a letter which was not preserved as a part of the New Testament canon. This is mentioned in 1 Corinthians 5:9-11.

Additional reports of poor conduct prompted another letter, referred to as 1 Corinthians. There was sexual immorality in the church and church members were taking fellow members to court, among other issues. One of the "other issues" was the manner in which the Corinthians were operating in the gifts of the Holy Spirit.

Beginning in chapter 12 of his epistle, Paul outlines the gifts of the Spirit, followed by the great chapter on love (13). Then in chapter 14, Paul gives instructions on the proper order for the gifts, particularly the vocal gifts, to be used when the church came together.

The gifts of the Spirit listed in chapter 12 are as follows:

The Revelation Gifts

1. The Word of Wisdom
2. The Word of Knowledge
3. Discerning of Spirits

The Vocal Gifts

1. Prophecy
2. Different Kinds of Tongues
3. Interpretation of Tongues

The Power Gifts

1. Faith
2. Gifts of Healing
3. Working of Miracles

For the purpose of this book, we will be dealing primarily with the vocal gifts and Paul's instructions for their use in chapter 14.

In chapter 13, Paul lists of the attributes of agape love:

1. Love suffers long
2. Love is kind
3. Love does not envy
4. Love does not parade itself
5. Love is not puffed up
6. Love does not behave rudely
7. Love does not seek its own
8. Love is not provoked
9. Love thinks no evil

10. Love does not rejoice in iniquity
11. Love rejoices in the truth
12. Love bears all things
13. Love believes all things
14. Love hopes all things
15. Love endures all things Love never fails

As the old song asks: "What's love got to do with it?!" Everything. Our singular motive for operating in the supernatural gifts of the Spirit is love.

Paul stated this emphatically in chapter 13:

> **1 Though I speak with the tongues of men and of angels, but have not love, I have become sounding brass or a clanging cymbal.**
> **2 And though I have the gift of prophecy, and understand all mysteries and all knowledge, and though I have all faith, so that I could remove mountains, but have not love, I am nothing.**

Tongues, prophecy, faith, without love behind it, means nothing. If an individual wants to be used by God, speaking in the assembly by the vocal gifts of the Spirit, selfish ambition must be rooted out and love be the only motivator.

Paul begins the 14th chapter with this reminder:

Pursue love

1 Corinthians 14 Section One (1-11)

14:1 Pursue love, and desire spiritual gifts, but especially that you may prophesy.

Chapter 13 deals with operating in love. Paul says to desire spiritual gifts, but pursue them in love. Chapter 12 outlined nine gifts of the Holy Spirit and chapter 13 emphasized love as our motivation.

In fact, when Paul closes his comments about the different gifts of the Spirit, he says this:

> **12:31 But earnestly desire the best gifts. And yet I show you a more excellent way.**

A more excellent way, or method to function in these supernatural gifts. It must be understood that a person could easily get puffed up in pride when used by God with healings, miracles, prophecy, or even tongues and interpretation. Keeping our motives pure is the only way to prevent this from happening. I'm reminded of one famous preacher who relayed the following. He had just preached an inspiring sermon to thousands of people and as he was leaving the premises in his car, he looked to his wife and asked, "How many truly great preachers do you think there are?" She responded, "One less than you think."

Here in chapter 14, Paul comes back to the gifts and the practical aspects of their operation. It's important to remember that the Bible was not written in chapters and verses. These were added later.

Paul places a priority on prophecy in our desire of spiritual gifts. As we go forward in our lesson, we will talk more about the gift of prophecy and define it further.

WORD GEMS

- "Pursue" (Gr. dioko) means "to run swiftly in order to catch, to press forward."
- "Love" (Gr. *agape*) means "the God-kind of love."
- "Desire" (Gr. *zeloo*) means "to burn with zeal; to desire earnestly; to be zealous in pursuit of."

14:2 For he who speaks in a tongue does not speak to men but to God, for no one understands him; however, in the spirit he speaks mysteries.

Here, Paul explains that tongues, for the individual believer, are not to be spoken for man's hearing, but God's. This differs from *tongues and interpretation* (which is the equivalent of prophecy). This verse disproves the myth that speaking in tongues are only for the purpose of preaching the gospel in another language. The Word of God clearly says, "no one understands him."

When one prays in tongues, he is speaking from his spirit (where the Holy Spirit lives) and is uttering mysteries to his own intellect. These mysteries are the will of God, unknown to the natural mind. This thought is conveyed in Romans 8:

> **Romans 8:26-28**
> **26 Likewise the Spirit also helps in our weaknesses. For we do not know what we should pray for as we ought, but the Spirit Himself makes intercession for us with groanings which cannot be uttered.**
> **27 Now He who searches the hearts knows what the mind of the Spirit is, because He makes intercession for the saints according to the will of God.**
> **28 And we know that all things work together for good to those who love God, to those who are the called according to His purpose.**

The "groanings which cannot be uttered" are referring to articulate speech. This is the Holy Spirit praying through us, the perfect will of God. When we pray in the spirit, the Holy Spirit is interceding through us. Our finite minds are limited to what we know, but the Holy Spirit in us is unlimited and knows all things. If we want "all things to work together for good," we need to allow the Holy Spirit to pray through us the hidden things that belong only to God.

Some Christians cannot stop living out of their intellect long enough to allow the Holy Spirit to lead them. The intellect was designed by God to be a servant to the spirit of man, not to be the dictator of our life.

- "Mysteries" (Gr. *mysterion*) means "hidden thing, secret, mystery; not obvious to the understanding."

14:3 But he who prophesies speaks edification and exhortation and comfort to men.

The simple gift of prophecy is not for prediction, but for edification, exhortation and comfort. Further, prophecy, outside of the apostolic ministry of the early church, is not inspired in the same way as Scripture. God is no longer adding to His Word. Further, the Corinthian church was prophesying by the Spirit and none of it was included in the Scripture, even though it was during the same time as the New Testament was being inspired.

Listed below are some of the components of New Testament prophecy:

- Prophesied about by the prophet Joel in the Old Testament (Joel 2:29). He said that both sons and daughters would prophesy.
- As noted, prophecy is for edification, edification and comfort.
- Prophecy is a supernatural insight or revelation from God, spoken in a known language.
- Prophecy is fallible (1 Corinthians 13:9).
- Prophecy is subject to Scripture.
- Prophecy does not add to the Word of God, but rather confirms it.

- If prophecy involves prediction, the word of wisdom is also in use.
- Prophecy should be desired and Paul wishes every Christian had the gift.
- When a person gives a prophecy, it must be done by faith (Romans 12:6).
- Prophecy should be judged by leadership.
- Prophecy should not be despised (1 Thessalonians 5:20.

Additionally, because one prophesies does not make him a prophet. One is a gift and the other is an office. As Paul stated in verse one, all believers should desire to prophesy.

From a practical standpoint, a person does not need to speak in King James English in order to give a prophetic word. I might add that God does not need to be spoken of in the first person (e.g., "I, the Lord, say…"), although at times, the Spirit may direct such. My point here is that we must separate Pentecostal tradition from actual Scripture. A prophecy may flow as follows: "The Lord has shown me that some here are in a state of fear and worry; the Lord would have you know that…"

WORD GEMS

- "Edification" (Gr. *oikodome*) means "the act of building up." This is a compound word with *oiko* meaning "house" and *doma* meaning "to build."
- "Exhortation" (Gr. *paraklesis*) means "called alongside to help." This is the same word used of the Holy Spirit in John 14:16.

- "Comfort" (Gr. *paramythia*) means "to calm, console, encourage."

14:4 He who speaks in a tongue edifies himself, but he who prophesies edifies the church.

Once more, Paul compares and contrasts tongues (without interpretation) and prophecy. This is a theme throughout the chapter. Understanding this distinction is a key to rightly dividing this chapter.

Tongues (without interpretation) edifies or builds up the believer (the speaker). Going back to verse 2, it must be known that Paul is referring to praying in tongues here in verse 4. Jude v. 20 tells us that one is built up in his most holy faith by praying in the Holy Spirit. Praying in tongues is likened unto charging one's spiritual batteries.

Some who oppose praying in tongues would have us believe that to edify one's self is of no value. However, how can we help others if we are not built up in the Lord? I have found that when I am praying in tongues a lot in my personal devotion that I am more sensitive to the leading of the Holy Spirit during times of ministry.

When a Christian gets baptized with the Holy Spirit and receives the gift of tongues, it should not be a one-time experience or a rarely used gift. The difference between the personal gift of tongues and the public gift of tongues (with interpretation) is that the latter may be exercised whenever desired, while the former may only be exercised as the Spirit wills.

Prophecy, on the other hand, edifies or builds up the church (the hearers). The nature of prophecy is defined in verse 3 and will be discussed at greater length as we move through the chapter.

In addition to the "thus saith the Lord" type of prophecy, there is a mantle of prophetic preaching that God wants to go forth from the pulpit. When preaching the Word, more often than not, I enter a place in the anointing where I no longer think about what I'm going to say next; it just pours forth from the Spirit. I am keenly aware, during those times, that I am speaking prophetically. It's almost as if you are outside of yourself while it occurs.

WORD GEMS

- "Unknown" is added by the translators because of the context.
- "Church" (Gr. *ekklesia*) means "called out ones." The church is made up of those who are called out from the world and unto Jesus.

14:5 I wish you all spoke with tongues, but even more that you prophesied; for he who prophesies is greater than he who speaks with tongues, unless indeed he interprets, that the church may receive edification.

Although some try to use verses from chapter 14 to minimize or entirely negate the gift of tongues, Paul makes it clear that all should speak with tongues.

There are three clear-cut examples in the book of Acts of speaking with tongues:

1. Acts 2 on the day of Pentecost: All 120 spoke in tongues
2. Acts 10 at Cornelius' house: All spoke in tongues
3. Acts 19 in Ephesus: All 12 spoke in tongues

In each example, 100% of the people spoke in tongues. If the gift was not for all Christians, why wouldn't there have been some who didn't receive? I realize that there are various hindrances to receiving the gift. Some of them are rooted in Pentecostal tradition. Other times, it's simply a mental block. At the end of this book, there are some tips that may help someone who has had difficulty receiving the gift of tongues.

In verse five, the first mention of tongues deals with *praying* in tongues with no interpretation needed. The second reference is the gifts of tongues with interpretation, to be done publicly in the church. This would be the equivalent of prophecy. So, if prophecy was a dime then tongues and interpretation would be two nickels; in either case, it would equal ten cents.

Paul indicates that as much as he wants everyone to speak in tongues, he wants them to have the gift of prophecy even more. Prophecy edifies and builds up others. He is not saying that I want you to have the gift of prophecy In place of tongues, but in addition to tongues.

In verses 4 and 5, Paul begins to set forth proper order for the vocal gifts of tongues/interpretation and prophecy. Further, he gives instruction on the difference between public tongues and private tongues (prayer).

WORD GEMS

- "Would" (Gr. *thelo*) means "to will, have in mind, intend." It is God's will for His children to speak in tongues.
- "Spoke" (Gr. *laleo*) means "to utter a voice or sound."
- "Greater" (Gr. *meizon*) means "stronger, greater in weight."

14:6 But now, brethren, if I come to you speaking with tongues, what shall I profit you unless I speak to you either by revelation, by knowledge, by prophesying, or by teaching?

Praying in tongues in front of an audience of people will not profit or benefit them. There may be times in an actual prayer meeting when praying out loud in tongues is appropriate, but this is for God's ears, not the peoples. An example of this is found in Acts 10 when Cornelius' entire household spoke in tongues aloud without interpretation.

Paul outlines the different types of verbal edification that should be happening in a church gathering:

- Revelation: The supernatural unveiling of truth. There is a difference between the intellectual understanding of the Word and the revelation knowledge that comes from the Holy Spirit.

- Knowledge: This is spiritual knowledge as well as the supernatural gift of the word of knowledge.
- Prophesying: Speaking by the Spirit unto edification, exhortation and comfort. This can also be through tongues and interpretation.
- Teaching: This is doctrine, the teaching of the Word of God. Every congregation needs the sound and anointed teaching of the Word of God in order to spiritually grow.

WORD GEMS

- Profit" (Gr. *opheleo*) means "to assist, to be useful or advantageous."

14:7 Even things without life, whether flute or harp, when they make a sound, unless they make a distinction in the sounds, how will it be known what is piped or played? 8 For if the trumpet makes an uncertain sound, who will prepare for battle?

Just as there is a distinction to natural sounds, there is a spiritual distinction between the sounds of praying in tongues and a message in tongues; likewise, there is a difference between simple preaching and speaking prophetically. Sometimes, it takes what I call "time under the anointing" to be able to distinguish the differences. This is why God places leaders in the body to judge or discern what is from the Holy Spirit and what is not (v. 29).

Two preachers can speak the exact same message, verbatim, but the source and the results are completely different. This can be true even if the message is spoken to the same group of people. That which is born of the flesh (intellect) is flesh and that which is born of the Spirit (anointing) is Spirit (John 3:6). Further, the flesh profits nothing; it is the Spirit who gives life (John 6:63).

Jesus said, "He who has an ear to hear, let him hear (Mark 4:9). He was not referring to physical hearing. Some Christians listen to sermons that are not anointed week after week, but they've never been exposed to the anointing of God to know the difference.

WORD GEMS

- "Distinction" (Gr. *diastole*) means "distinction, difference; of the different sounds musical instruments make."
- "Known" (Gr. *ginosko*) means "to know, understand, perceive, have knowledge of."
- "Uncertain" (Gr. *adelos*) means "indistinct, uncertain, obscure."

14:9 So likewise you, unless you utter by the tongue words easy to understand, how will it be known what is spoken? For you will be speaking into the air.

While the point that Paul is making deals with tongues versus a known language, we can also state that even when speaking in a known language, one should endeavor to make the presentation easy to understand. Too many parade their knowledge in front of the church while no one is being edified. As I often say, if no one is learning then no one is teaching.

Sometimes I read books or articles that are so verbose and filled with minutia. It really becomes hard to get to understand the point being made. The same is true when someone lectures or speaks. The purpose, too often, is to impress the audience with one's knowledge and/or oratory skills. The ministry of Jesus, however, presents a much different model. He spoke in simple terms so that people could understand.

I took the words of Jesus from the Sermon on the Mount (Matthew 5 from the NKJV) and ran them through a readability test. Next, I took a popular Bible Commentary written about the same passage of Scripture and compared the results. The words of Jesus were on a grade level* of 6.6 and the commentary about the words of Jesus was on a grade level of 14.2. The reading ease** of the words of Jesus was 80.1 (on a scale of 100) and the commentary's was 47.8.

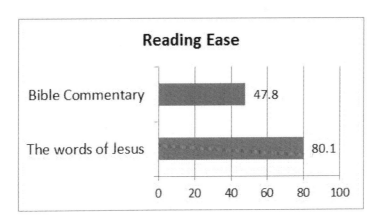

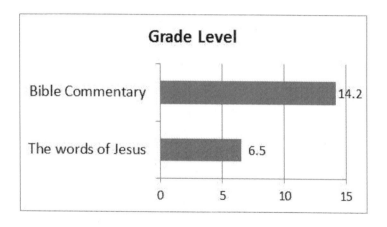

* Flesch Reading Scale
** Flesch-Kincaid Grade Level

This should alert us to the need to simplify our presentations in order to be understood.

WORD GEMS

- "Understand" (Gr. *eusemos*) means "well marked, clear, definite, distinct."

14:10 There are, it may be, so many kinds of languages in the world, and none of them is without significance. 11 Therefore, if I do not know the meaning of the language, I shall be a foreigner to him who speaks, and he who speaks will be a foreigner to me.

All languages have their own importance. Each having unique expressions, colloquialisms, slang, etc. However, if the hearer does not know the language or understand these meanings, there is no value to the hearer.

The Bible itself has been translated into over 2,500 languages. The Summer Institute of Linguistics has catalogued approximately 7,000 distinct languages in the world today. Unrelated to these two verses, but pertinent to our overall topic, when a believer speaks in tongues, it could be one of these 7,000 languages or even a tongue of angels (1 Corinthians 13:1). There are many times that I recognize distinct changes in the tongue I am speaking.

WORD GEMS

- "World" (Gr. *kosmos*) means "the inhabitants of the earth, men, the human family."
- "Barbarian" (Gr. *barbaros*) means "one who speaks a foreign or strange language which is not understood by the hearer."

1 Corinthians 14 Section Two (12-17)

14:12 Even so you, since you are zealous for spiritual gifts, let it be for the edification of the church that you seek to excel.

Paul does not want to squash the zeal that the Corinthians have for spiritual gifts. Instead, he wants them to be zealous for the right reasons. The motive for all spiritual gifts is the edification of the church.

I have been in some churches where there was such a spirit of control in the area of spiritual manifestations that the Holy Spirit had no freedom to move. In that type of atmosphere, people are not zealous for spiritual gifts, but rather fearful of them. I tell my church that if you feel like God wants to use you in the gifts, just step out; if you make a mistake, but your motives are right, we will use it as a learning opportunity. I never want people to be fearful of the manifestation of the Spirit. Everyone has to start somewhere.

It should be noted that the zeal spoken of here has nothing to do with the spirit of competition. We should not want spiritual gifts for personal notoriety. The singular purpose of the gifts is the edification of the body of Christ.

Before seeking the Lord for spiritual gifts, check your motives towards other people. Do you seek the blessing of others above yourself? That's a hard question. But that's what God is looking for when we lay our lives down to be used by Him. Some seek to build their ministry through the gifts of the Spirit, but Paul said that the gifts were for the building up of others.

WORD GEMS

- "Zealous" (Gr. *zelotes*) means "one with burning zeal; most eagerly desirous; to vehemently contend for a thing."
- "Gifts" is added by the translators based on the context.
- "Excel" (Gr. *perisseuo*) means "to superabound, to be in excess, to overflow."

14:13 Therefore let him who speaks in a tongue pray that he may interpret.

The companion gift of interpretation of tongues should be prayed for by everyone who speaks in tongues. The first thing that stands out here is that Paul is informing believers that they should pray for the gifts of the Spirit. Secondly, we should pray with wisdom. If you have tongues, pray to interpret. If someone needs healing, pray for the gifts of healing, not the word of wisdom. The best gift is the one that's needed the most in a particular situation.

The gift of the interpretation of tongues is the supernatural interpretation of what has been spoken in an unknown tongue. To be clear, this gift is not a *translation* of that tongue, but an interpretation. The tongue may be two minutes in length, but the interpretation only 10 words.

Sometimes God gives you the entire message before you speak it and other times just a word or two, which must be spoken out in faith before the Spirit gives you more.

When you pray in tongues and you also receive an interpretation, it pulls back the veil on the hidden things of God – the mysteries spoken of in verse two.

WORD GEMS

- "Pray" (Gr. proseuchomai) means "to earnestly make supplication for."

14:14 For if I pray in a tongue, my spirit prays, but my understanding is unfruitful.

Notice that Paul writes, "If I pray in a tongue." Some have mistakenly believed that tongues are only for public use (such as declaring the gospel) and must be accompanied by interpretation. In Acts chapter two, when the disciples spoke in tongues, everyone present heard in their own native language the wonderful works of God (Acts 2:4-11). But when you examine the other two examples of tongues in the Book of Acts, this was not the case; tongues were spoken without interpretation or understanding by the hearers.

However, here Paul is talking about praying. Speaking to God, not to men. He also addressed this in verse two. When one is praying in tongues, where is the prayer coming from? He said, "my *spirit* prays." The Holy Spirit live in the born again spirit. He that is "joined to the Lord is one spirit" (1 Corinthians 6:17).

What does it mean when it says, "my understanding is unfruitful?" Remember, tongues come from the spirit not the mind. Tongues are utterance given by the Holy Spirit. The natural mind of man, the faculties of the intellect, cannot manufacture the supernatural manifestation of God.

One will be edified in spirit and strengthened in faith by praying in tongues even if there is no understanding to the mind. However, as Paul stated in verse 13, pray for interpretation. This will allow one to pray in the spirit and the understanding.

As a reminder: personal/private tongues do NOT require an interpretation; public tongues spoken before the church always requires an interpretation.

Private Tongues	Public Tongues
Does not require an interpretation, even though one may be given	Always requires an interpretation

WORD GEMS

- "Understanding" (Gr. nous) means "the mind, comprised of the faculties of perceiving and understanding; the intellectual faculties."

14:15 What is the conclusion then? I will pray with the spirit, and I will also pray with the understanding. I will sing with the spirit, and I will also sing with the understanding.

Should a Christian pray in tongues or in their understanding? Simply stated, both. Of course, in the context of this passage, Paul is referring to praying with the Spirit-given interpretation of the tongue. This is a tremendous benefit that aids one in praying the will of God. This is not to say that one cannot pray in tongues unless he has the interpretation, for the interpretation is as the Spirit wills. One cannot force an interpretation or conjure one up. For this reason, pray and ask God to give you the interpretation.

I do not always have an interpretation for each time I pray in tongues. There are times when I only know the general area that I am praying about and other times when I do not know at all. But it's a tremendous blessing when God provides the exact interpretation.

This verse also underscores another important principle: there are different kinds of prayer. For instance, there is the *prayer of faith* that should be prayed when the will of God is known through His Word. Another kind of prayer is the *prayer of consecration* when the will of God is not known. Here in this verse, we see two additional kinds of prayer.

Further, Paul said that we can sing with the spirit and with the understanding. The same principles apply. I have a terrible voice in the natural, but when I'm singing in the spirit I can almost keep a tune.

- See "Understanding" above.

14:16 Otherwise, if you bless with the spirit, how will he who occupies the place of the uninformed say "Amen" at your giving of thanks, since he does not understand what you say? 17 For you indeed give thanks well, but the other is not edified.

Paul explains that if one invokes a blessing in tongues upon another who is uninformed that the uninformed will not be edified.   This is simple common sense. Concerning the uniformed person, the Amplified translation renders it this way: "How can anyone in the position of an outsider or he who is not gifted with [interpreting of unknown] tongues…"

Note that Paul said in verse 17 that in and of itself, blessing with the spirit (or in tongues) is giving thanks well; however, the uninformed hearer is not edified. Some may want to question, "How does a person know that he is giving thanks when speaking in tongues?" Simple answer: because the Bible says so. If you remember, when the Holy Spirit fell in Cornelius' house, this is what the Bible says happened:

> **Acts 10:44-46**
> **44 While Peter was still speaking these words, the Holy Spirit fell upon all those who heard the word.**
> **45 And those of the circumcision who believed were astonished, as many as came with Peter, because the**

gift of the Holy Spirit had been poured out on the Gentiles also.

46 For they heard them speak with tongues and magnify God.

These folks were speaking in tongues and magnifying God. It doesn't say that there was interpretation, yet they knew that God was being magnified. As believers, we have an anointing within who teaches us all things (1 John 2:27).

WORD GEMS

- "Uninformed" (Gr. *idotes*) meaning "ignorant, unlearned." This is the word that our English word "idiot" is derived from.

1 Corinthians 14 Section Three (18-25)

14:18 I thank my God I speak with tongues more than you all;

The Corinthian church was speaking in tongues a lot. A whole lot! One person I know claims that the Corinthians were speaking in pagan babble. If so, why does Paul never come out and say that? Further, why does he give them instructions on how and when to do it? And lastly, Paul says in verse 18 that he speaks in tongues more than all of them! The Amplified translations says, "more than all of you put together."

How anyone can claim that Paul was making the case for cessation of tongues or that the tongues in reference were pagan babble is beyond my ability to grasp. Paul clearly states his personal experience with tongues. When you couple verse 18 with verse 19 it's easy to see that the case Paul is making is the distinction between private and public tongues.

There are lots of reasons that believers should pray in tongues. Below, I have listed a few of them.

Reasons for praying in tongues:

1. *Tongues are the initial sign of the Baptism with the Holy Spirit (Mark 16:17; Acts 2:1-4).*

   Tongues are a supernatural sign of the indwelling presence of the Holy Spirit. This begs the question, "If one does not have the gift of tongues, is he baptized with the Holy Spirit?" My answer to this is no. This does not mean that the person is not saved; nor does it mean that the Holy Spirit is not living in the person. But, according to the Bible, the person who has not received the gift of tongues has not received the baptism with the Holy Spirit, as described in the Book of Acts. The Baptism with the Holy Spirit is not the same thing as when the Holy Spirit baptizes us into the Body of Christ. That is our salvation experience. The Baptism with the Holy Spirit is our empowerment for service.

2. *Praying in tongues edifies and builds up the believer (1 Corinthians 14:4; Jude 20).*

   Think of praying in the Spirit as recharging your spiritual batteries. Jude verse 20 says that we build ourselves up. Being in this world takes a lot out of a believer. Hebrews 2:1 tells us that we are leaking vessels, and as such, we need to stay filled up.

3. *Praying in tongues allows us to pray the perfect will of God (Romans 8:26-28).*

   We are weak in our own ability, but the Holy Spirit is our Helper. He makes intercession on our behalf when we pray in tongues. The Holy Spirit knows the perfect will of God in every situation. The human mind can only know what has been revealed. If we limit our prayers to that which has already been revealed, we limit the Holy Spirit from working in our lives as He desires.

4. *Praying in tongues allows for you to pray for the unknown (1 Corinthians 14:2).*

   The word translated mysteries in 14:2 means, "hidden thing, secret counsel."

5. *Praying in tongues give one boldness to witness for Christ (Acts 1:8).*

   Jesus said in Acts 1:8 that after you receive the baptism with Holy Spirit, you would receive power to be witnesses unto Him.

WORD GEMS

- "All" (Gr. pas) means "all collectively or put together."

14:19 yet in the church I would rather speak five words with my understanding, that I may teach others also, than ten thousand words in a tongue.

Even though praying in tongues is so beneficial that Paul does it more than the entire Corinthian church put together, it doesn't serve anyone to do so in a public meeting without interpretation.

The emphasis here is on teaching, not on personal edification. It's important to pray much in the spirit prior to the meeting. This stirs up the gifts and anointing and prepares one for ministry. Sometimes just prior to teaching, if there is something that occurs that is distracting (e.g., technical difficulties), I will pray in tongues the entire time, under my breath, in order to maintain the focus of the Spirit.

Some have mistakenly used this verse to say that tongues aren't needed in the assembly. They are failing to recognize Paul's desire to teach the difference between private tongues in prayer and public tongues with interpretation. To stand before a congregation and speak in tongues with no interpretation is only edifying to the speaker; the hearers are not edified.

WORD GEMS

- "Understanding" (Gr. *nous*) means "the mind, comprised of the faculties of perceiving and understanding; the intellectual faculties."
- "Teach" (Gr. *katecheo*) means "to teach orally, to instruct."

14:20 Brethren, do not be children in understanding; however, in malice be babes, but in understanding be mature.

Paul previously said in chapter 12 to not be ignorant of spiritual gifts. Here, again in chapter 14, he emphasizes the need for understanding on the subject of spiritual gifts in the assembly. The type of understanding that Paul is speaking of is not an intellectual understanding of spiritual gifts. He is speaking of a spiritual understanding (see the word meaning below). Men such as John MacArthur may attack believers who operate in the gifts of the Spirit, but he does so from an intellectual standpoint. In doing so, he reveals his spiritual ignorance.

The Bible warns us that the Scriptures can be twisted to our own harm. Peter specifically warned this about some of Paul's writings.

> **2 Peter 3:15-16**
> **15 and consider that the longsuffering of our Lord is salvation—as also our beloved brother Paul, according to the wisdom given to him, has written to you,**
> **16 as also in all his epistles, speaking in them of these things, in which are some things hard to understand, which untaught and unstable people twist to their own destruction, as they do also the rest of the Scriptures.**

Here is verse 20, Paul compares and contrasts spiritual understanding with malice. In the area of malice, God's people are to be like babes – innocent. The gifts of the Spirit are not to be abused for the purpose of injuring someone spiritually, emotionally or financially. I have witnessed these abuses within the church and parachurch mine ministries for years. "Thus saith the Lord..." for the purpose of personal gain at someone else's loss.

In our understanding of the things Paul is discussing, God wants us to be mature. The time has come for many to be teachers, but instead they need re-taught the basics.

- "Children" (Gr. *paidion*) means "infant, just recently born."
- "Understanding" is a different original word than in previous uses (nous) in this chapter (Gr. phren) and means "the faculty of perceiving from the heart." The word is not dealing with the intellect, but with spiritual understanding.
- "Mature" (Gr. *teleios*) means "wanting nothing necessary to completeness."

14:21 In the law it is written:

"With men of other tongues and other lips
I will speak to this people;
And yet, for all that, they will not hear Me,"

Paul quotes Isaiah 28:11-12 here. This is the fifth and last Old Testament prophecy fulfilled in 1 Corinthians. This prophecy reveals that God intended over 700 years before Christ to speak to men with stammering lips and other tongues.

A part of the passage in Isaiah that Paul did not quote deals with the rest that tongues provide:

> **To whom He said, "This is the rest with which**
> **You may cause the weary to rest,"**
> **And, "This is the refreshing"**

Praying in tongues gives the believer a refreshing in the spirit. As long as we are in this world, we will have opportunity to get weary. This wonderful gift from God helps to lift us up above the weariness.

WORD GEMS

- The quoted passage in Isaiah uses the word "rest" in 28:12. This word (*mnuwchah*) means "peaceful, comfortable, quiet." Praying in tongues allows the believer to enter this type of rest.

14:22 Therefore tongues are for a sign, not to those who believe but to unbelievers; but prophesying is not for unbelievers but for those who believe.

Tongues are a sign for unbelievers. This is the miracle of Pentecost. This sign arrested the hearts of 3,000 men on the day that the church was born. Further, tongues were the sign that the Holy Spirit had been given to the Gentiles, just as He had to the Jews in Acts chapter 10, at Cornelius' house.

Prophecy, on the other hand, is for believers. Notice that he doesn't use the word "sign" with regards to believers. As believers, we do not need signs, as such. We understand that prophecy is for our edification and is given by God for the building up of the body. But God's primary way of speaking to His children for direction is through the indwelling Holy Spirit.

Some believers are always waiting on a "sign from God" before they will obey what God has already placed on their hearts. If you remember, God gave the Israelites a sign every day for 40 years. There was a cloud by day and a fire by night 24 hours a day. This was to designate the presence of God. God also gave them manna from heaven every morning. Yet, they all died in unbelief. Their carcasses fell in the wilderness.

WORD GEMS

- "Sign" (Gr. *semeion*) means "to make known through a supernatural event."

14:23 Therefore if the whole church comes together in one place, and all speak with tongues, and there come in those who are uninformed or unbelievers, will they not say that you are out of your mind?

To start with, notice that the whole church should be coming together in one place. There is a great decline in church attendance in America. God's people need one another and our communities need the church to be a light to their cities.

Also, notice that Paul's scenario has everyone speaking in tongues, not just a few chosen ones. It is God's will for every believer to receive the baptism with the Holy Spirit and the gift of praying in tongues. Just not all at the same time in the assembly!

This verse deals with three groups of people:

1. The church
2. The uninformed

3. The unbelievers

Leaders within the church need to be aware that all three groups will be represented in every single worship gathering. At The River, where I pastor, we have first-time guests every single Sunday. The key ingredient to make people feel welcome is the love of God shown through His people. People are already stepping out of their comfort zones just by attending. There's no need to try to give them an experience that is just like where they are coming from. They are there because something is broken in their lives and they are seeking for something that is currently lacking.

Sadly, in many churches today, these three groups look the same. And that's the way some churches like it. But there is nothing wrong with folks getting uncomfortable. That's the conviction of the Holy Spirit. I was uncomfortable the night I got saved.

Let's look at how the Amplified translation renders this verse:

> Therefore, if the whole church assembles and all of you speak in [unknown] tongues, and the ungifted and uninitiated or unbelievers come in, will they not say that you are demented?

Paul's instructions are very clear and stated in an obvious way here. Everyone should not be speaking in tongues at the same time in the open assembly. Certainly, there are some Pentecostal churches that fail to follow these instructions. Some Christians believe that people cannot control what happens when the Spirit is moving. But the Word of God is very clear on this matter and the Holy Spirit is the author of the Word; He will not contradict Himself.

Let's look beyond the immediate instruction and talk about how these folks, who are not familiar with the manifestations of the Spirit can get acclimated. I will start with the ungifted and uninitiated, or as the NKJV translates it, the uninformed. There should be teaching on the gifts of the Spirit, including tongues and interpretation. If someone is uninformed, the best thing to do is to inform him. This can be done in a non-threatening way. Dragging someone to the altar and having a group of people praying in tongues all around them will only serve to freak that person out! Teach... teach... teach from the Word of God. And certainly do not do so apologetically, as if you are sorry to offend them. Do not be ashamed of the Holy Spirit or His presence and gifts. However, people simply need to learn. And, as stated in this verse, it's important to set the right model in front of them.

As for unbelievers, those who aren't saved, leadership must ensure that things are done decently and in order, but leaders should not water down or quench the Holy Spirit in efforts to make the church "user friendly" or "seeker sensitive." In the coming verses, we will see why.

WORD GEMS

- "Out of your mind" (Gr. *mainomai*) means "to rave as a maniac."

14:24 But if all prophesy, and an unbeliever or an uninformed person comes in, he is convinced by all, he is convicted by all.

All have the ability to prophesy. To prophesy does not make one a prophet. The former is a gift and the latter is an office.

People usually think that "prophecy" means to predict (foretell) what will happen in the future. This is frequently confused because people fail to understand that there is a difference between the simple gift of prophecy and the office of a prophet. Prophecy in the New Testament church carried no prediction with it whatsoever, for "he that prophesies speaks unto men to edification, and exhortation, and comfort" (1 Corinthians 14:3).

- Edification
- Exhortation
- Comfort

Prophecy is divinely inspired and anointed utterance; a supernatural proclamation in a known language. It is the manifestation of the Spirit of God - not of the human intellect.

Prophecy does not come from the mind of man, but from the Spirit of God. As with all nine gifts, it is "as the Spirit wills" (1 Corinthians 12:11) and not as man wills.

Scripture tells us that prophecy within the church should be judged (1 Corinthians 14:29). If it doesn't line up to the Word of God, it should be rejected.

There are different types of prophecy, so to speak. Perhaps, *levels* would be a better word than *type*. To explain, let's look at the purpose of prophecy in the context of this verse. The goal is to convince the uninformed and/or the unbeliever. In other words, for those outside of the church family who are in attendance, to be convicted. Where does conviction come from? The Holy Spirit (John 16:7-11).

In a meeting, there may be corporate worship and near the end, one to three members of the congregation who speak out a word of prophecy (edification, exhortation and comfort) to the body. From the leadership comes some sort of confirmation to indicate that the messages were from the Holy Spirit. This is one type or level of prophecy.

Further, there is prophetic preaching from the Holy Spirit that goes far beyond a sermon outline. I have come to experience this more and more the past few years. When this is occurring, the Holy Spirit is putting the words in your mouth just before you speak them. They are not coming from the intellect or the piece of paper lying on the pulpit. After the meeting, the prophetic ministry is confirmed by numerous people who say that it was just like God was speaking directly to them.

The church, as a whole, really suffers from the lack of prophetic preaching. Pastors go to seminary and get their minds pumped full of knowledge, and in many cases, unbelief. Further, the congregation gets so accustomed to hearing these types of sermons that they don't know the difference between the anointing and head knowledge.

- "Convinced" (Gr. *elencho*) means "to rebuke, admonish, refute."
- "Convicted" (Gr. *anakrino*) means "to scrutinize, to sift, to investigate." The word is a compound word with *ana* (the preposition) meaning "in the midst" and *krino* meaning "judge." The implication is that the Holy Spirit is judging the heart of the person from within.

14:25 And thus the secrets of his heart are revealed; and so, falling down on his face, he will worship God and report that God is truly among you.

The result of such anointed prophetic ministry is that the uninformed and unbeliever will have the secrets of their hearts exposed and know that only God could do this and they will fall down in repentance. This is the difference between ministry from the intellect and ministry from the Spirit. Churning out Bible lessons with no anointing will not produce life-changing results. I once saw a book titled, "Instant Sermons for Busy Pastors." It made me sick to my stomach.

People are seeking for what is real. Unbelievers can spot phony a mile away. Salt that has lost its savor is only good to be walked on. It is not enough to have a "performance" down perfect. The best music and the best orator cannot save or heal anyone. If what is described in verse 25 is not happening in your church then the Holy Spirit is not in control. He is being quenched by mad-made efforts to push religion.

- "Secrets" (Gr. *kryptos*) means "private, hidden, inwardly secret."
- "Revealed" (Gr. *phaneros*) means "to be made apparent, manifest, plainly recognized."
- "Worship" (Gr. *proskyneo*) means "to prostrate oneself in homage and reverence."
- "Truly" (Gr. *ontos*) means "certainty, in point of fact."

1 Corinthians 14 Section Four (26-33)

14:26 How is it then, brethren? Whenever you come together, each of you has a psalm, has a teaching, has a tongue, has a revelation, has an interpretation. Let all things be done for edification.

Again, we see that the instructions being given are for "whenever we come together." A worship gathering of the church should not be scripted to the point that the Holy Spirit cannot manifest through His people. This is not to say that there shouldn't be order.

Often, people will approach me just before a meeting and say, "Can I share?" Normally, I ask the person how long do they think it will take. I ask this because as a leader, I'm responsible for the entire meeting. I need to be able to adjust the events that are scheduled if a testimony is going to take 15 minutes versus two or three. Everyone who shares also has a responsibility to limit the content to that which edifies. There are many things we could talk about, but in church, the focus is on edification. Church services that go on endlessly often happen because of rambles, announcements, and windy preachers who don't know when the anointing lifted. We blame the Holy Spirit for our lack of time management.

The point here is that when the brethren come together, it's not just as spectators. God's wants active participants. Here are the different manifestations or gifts listed in the verse:

- Psalm
- Teaching
- Tongue
- Revelation
- Interpretation

Paul wasn't trying to be exhaustive, but representative. Let's look at each of these and also incorporate our word gems:

WORD GEMS

- "Psalm" (Gr. *psalmos*) means "a spiritual song." God is able to give a prophetic word through song. Many of the great prophecies in Scripture were given through song.
- "Teaching" (Gr. *didache*) means "doctrine, instruction." The church needs to be a place of teaching and instruction in the Word of God. Doctrine is needed in order to be established in the Word.
- "Tongue" (Gr. *glossa*) means "a language or dialect." In the context of the New Testament, a tongue is a supernatural utterance from the Holy Spirit. If used publicly, it requires an interpretation.
- "Revelation" (Gr. *apokalypsis*) means "a disclosure of truth; to uncover or lay open what has been veiled or

covered up." God can give someone a revelation on a verse or passage of scripture that will bless and edify the entire body. Too often, God shows us something and we keep it to ourselves instead of sharing with the body.

- "Interpretation" (Gr. *hermeneia*) means "to explain in words, to expound." This spiritual gift is not a translation, but an interpretation. In addition to interpreting a tongue, there can be interpretation of dreams and visions.

Again, this list is representative. Other gifts of the Spirit are listed in the following locations:

- 1 Corinthians 12:8-11
- 1 Corinthians 12:28
- Romans 12:6-8
- Ephesians 4:11

Helps and administrations are listed among the spiritual gifts. These are not often looked upon as supernatural gifts, but, in fact, they are.

As Paul said, "Let all things be done for edification."

14:27 If anyone speaks in a tongue, let there be two or at the most three, each in turn, and let one interpret.

This is an interesting verse. When looking at the original Greek as well as various translations, it is difficult to determine whether Paul is limiting the number of messages or the number of *messengers*. "Each in turn" seems to indicate that he is referring to people.

From a practical standpoint, there really shouldn't be more than three messages in tongues, even if the intention is to limit the number of messengers. However, if it were to occur, I don't think that this verse would be violated.

I think that the way the New Living Translation renders it is accurate:

> No more than two or three should speak in tongues. They must speak one at a time, and someone must interpret what they say.

"Let one interpret." Again, this can be understood in more than one way. It could mean, only one person can be the interpreter for all three messages/messengers, or it could mean there is to be only one interpretation for each message. I am inclined to believe the latter. In other words, there should not be competing interpretations for a single message in tongues. Otherwise, there will be confusion.

Now, let's say that more than one person receives the interpretation. The two individuals are not likely to speak the exact same words if they were both to give the interpretation (remember, only one interpretation). The general message would be the same, but it may be said two different ways. How can this be? Remember, that the gospels of Matthew, Mark and Luke are basically telling the exact same story, but each are said differently even though all three are inspired by the Holy Spirit.

God uses each person's individuality with prophecy and interpretation.

WORD GEMS

- "Turn" (Gr. *meros*) means "one part of a whole." In other words, no one person has all that God wants to say. He or she is just a part of the whole.

14:28 But if there is no interpreter, let him keep silent in church, and let him speak to himself and to God.

"If there is no interpreter." How can one know if there is an interpreter? To start with, Paul is writing this to an established congregation. They have spent enough time together to know the various giftings in play within the congregation.

Further, pastors should have the gift of interpretation. I remember Lester Sumrall saying that his biggest concern when asked to pastor his first church was that he had never received the gift of interpretation. He accepted the position and the first Sunday there was a message in tongues and God immediately gave him the gift of interpretation. In our church services, God gives me interpretation to messages in tongues, but sometimes, I will allow someone else to be used. But as long as I am there, people know that there is an interpreter.

What should a person do if there is no interpreter? Paul says, "Let him keep silent." Not an ordinary silent though. He says, "Let him speak to himself and to God." It's important to note that the speaker has control over the tongue. The Holy Spirit is a gentleman and will not override anyone's mental or physical faculties.

The believer who is blessed with tongues has the ability to keep it to himself and to God. In other words, to pray so lightly under one's breath that no one around is even aware. I do this all the time. Not just in church but in the market place and everywhere I go. The volume control belongs to the person. The Holy Spirit does not control this for a person.

WORD GEMS

- "Silent" (Gr. sigao) means "to keep silent, keep close, be concealed."

I believe that the part about being concealed is the appropriate thought here.

14:29 Let two or three prophets speak, and let the others judge.

Here, Paul speaks specifically of the prophets, not just those who prophesy. At this time, let us define a prophet:

Prophets: There are three major realms of prophecy:

1. Prophecy of Scripture (1 Pet. 1:20-21). This level of prophecy is complete. All other prophecy must be judged by the Prophecy of Scripture.

2. The Office of the Prophet (I Cor. 12:28; Eph. 4:11). A prophet is someone who operates in the ministry gift of the prophet.
3. The Gift of Prophecy (I Cor. 12:10; 14:1, 3, 6). All believers are open to this manifestation of the Spirit. The gift must be operated within the guidelines of Scripture (I Cor. 14).

A prophet is used to give direction to the church. This is not a controlling directive, but a confirming one. At times, prophets will give direction to individuals, especially those in authority. The prophet Agabus is recorded as prophesying to both the corporate church and individuals:

- The church, Acts 11:27-29
- An individual (Paul), Acts 21:10-11.

A prophet's ministry involves revelation, confirmation and warning. The prophet's ministry is especially valuable in identifying and confirming ministry gifts within a presbytery setting (see Acts 13:1-3; I Tim. 4:14).

A prophet will operate in the gift of prophecy, as well as the word of knowledge, word of wisdom, and discerning of spirits. Simply operating in the gift of prophecy does not make one a prophet.

A genuine prophet's words will come to pass. There are many self-proclaimed prophets in the land who do not wish their words to be judged for accuracy. However, the Bible mandate is: "Let two or three prophets speak and let the others judge" (I

Cor. 14:29). A prophet who will not submit to authority and be accountable for his words is not to be heeded (see Deuteronomy 18:22).

Paul gives the instructions here in verse 29 that only two or three prophets should speak in any one meeting and that one should judge. The one who judges should be the ruling elder, in most cases, the position we call "pastor" in most churches.

The following are some guidelines to judge prophecy:

- **Does the giver of the prophesy have the fruit of a godly life?** Matthew 7:15-16 says: *Beware of false prophets, who come to you in sheep's clothing, but inwardly they are ravenous wolves. You will know them by their fruits.* Those who are being used in the prophetic gifting should have lives that are demonstrating fruit. This does not mean that they have to be perfect. Otherwise, God would never use anyone.

- **Does it line up to the Word of God?** If anything said in the prophecy conflicts or contradicts the Word, it is not from the Holy Spirit; He will never contradict Himself.

- **Does it glorify Jesus?** Revelation 19:10 says, "For the testimony of Jesus is the spirit of prophecy." Prophecy will not glorify a man, a ministry, a church, a movement or a denomination; it will glorify Jesus. John 16:14 says that the Holy Spirit has been sent to glorify Jesus.

- **Does it edify, exhort and/or comfort?** Paul was clear in verse three that these were the components of prophesy.

- **Does it come to pass?** If there are any elements of prediction within the word given, does the prediction come to pass? As previously noted, prediction would be part of the word of wisdom operating in conjunction with prophesy. This must be judged by leadership as well. I have heard many predictions over the years – some by famous preachers – that never came to pass.

- **Does the prophesy bear witness with leadership?** Those who are in place to judge the words given must have a witness in their spirit that the message was from God.

Prophecy is a beautiful gift in the church when proper checks and balances are in place to keep things in order.

WORD GEMS

- "Prophets" (Gr. *prophetes*) means "an inspire speaker who is moved by the Spirit of God."
- "Judge" (Gr. *diakrino*) means "to make a distinction, to discern."

14:30 But if anything is revealed to another who sits by, let the first keep silent.

No one person has the entire revelation of what God wants to say. There should be teamwork and cooperation in the flow of the Holy Spirit in a meeting. The church is Antioch in Acts chapter 13 is a great example.

> **Acts 13:1-3**
> **1 Now in the church that was at Antioch there were certain prophets and teachers: Barnabas, Simeon who was called Niger, Lucius of Cyrene, Manaen who had been brought up with Herod the tetrarch, and Saul.**
> **2 As they ministered to the Lord and fasted, the Holy Spirit said, "Now separate to Me Barnabas and Saul for the work to which I have called them."**
> **3 Then, having fasted and prayed, and laid hands on them, they sent them away.**

Paul's instructions in verse 30 are given to remove the spirit of competition among those who are gifted to lead and speak prophetically to the church. It should be understood that Paul is not saying that *everyone* should be given the chance to speak, but specifically those with the prophetic mantle.

I have seen numerous examples of churches that go without pastors on an intermittent basis. During these periods, members of the congregation will take turns speaking. If not careful, those people will take too much of a liking to the situation. This is a problem simply because if the calling and anointing is not there, no fruit will result.

The point I'm making is that the two or three who speak need to be called and anointed.

- "Revealed" (Gr. *apokalypto*) means "a disclosure of truth; to uncover or lay open what has been veiled or covered up."
- "Silent" (Gr. *sigao*) means "to keep silent, keep close, be concealed."

14:31 For you can all prophesy one by one, that all may learn and all may be encouraged.

"All" should be understood in relation to verse 29, meaning two or three. It is God's will that all learn and be encouraged. Aside from worship and fellowship, these are the two greatest reasons to come to the house of God: to learn and to be encouraged.

The word "learn" in this verse also carries the idea of learning by use and practice. I emphasize in our church all the time that you have to step out by faith to be used by the Spirit. Part of that process is learning on the job, so to speak. As long as one's motives are right, no one will ever be condemned for making a mistake in our church with the gifts of the Spirit. As Paul lovingly does with the Corinthians, as their spiritual father (1 Corinthians 4:15), we will give guidance and correction in order for the person to grow.

The purpose of the prophets speaking is to develop God's people through this learning model.

- "Learn" (Gr. *manthano*) means "to increase in knowledge, to learn by use and practice."
- "Encouraged" (Gr. *parakaleo*) means "called to one's side to help."

14:32 And the spirits of the prophets are subject to the prophets.

This small verse reveals a great spiritual principle. The Holy Spirit does nothing out of control. Further, He does not force or move through anyone against their will. If someone has a tongue or a prophecy, that person has the ability (and responsibility) to hold it until the appropriate time and place. If the time and place do not present themselves, it must be held. These are the very clear instructions that Paul gives throughout this chapter.

Examples:

- If there is no interpreter present, do not give a tongue.
- If someone is speaking from the pulpit, do not interrupt with a prophecy.
- If three people have already given a message in tongues, do not be the fourth.

We must not act foolishly or irresponsibly and then blame the Holy Spirit for our actions. This is what gives Spirit-filled Christians a bad reputation. It is the foolish acts of a few. Through solid teaching from the Word of God and proper leadership, the church can function in the supernatural power of

God and flow in the gifts of the Spirit. And things will be done correctly and in proper order.

WORD GEMS

- "Subject" (Gr. hypotasso) means "to subdue, be under obedience." This is a Greek military term.

14:33 For God is not the author of confusion but of peace, as in all the churches of the saints.

God is not the author of confusion! Why then is there confusion in the church? Because of the flesh and man's desire to be seen or put on a show. Sometimes it can also be due to ignorance or lack of teaching.

Let's understand that just because we don't understand something doesn't mean that it's "confusion" by default. This is the position that many cessationists take. God expects us to be educated in the manifestations of the Spirit. He told us not to be ignorant:

> *1 Corinthians 12:1 Now concerning spiritual gifts, brethren, I do not want you to be ignorant.*

What is cessationism? The following is a definition from Wikipedia:

In Christian theology, cessationism is the outworking of a three-fold belief-system:

1. That the Holy Spirit's purpose in imparting "sign gifts" has expired;
2. That the sign gifts (or "apostolic gifts') were given exclusively to the original twelve apostles, so that the sign gifts and Apostleship are inextricably linked;
3. That the position and/or gift of Apostleship no longer exists.

With this foundation, many cessationists argue that:

1. The sign gifts have ceased, and
2. The sign gifts are not expected to reappear. These sign gifts/Apostolic gifts are:
   a) Speaking in unlearned, real, human, languages, which are also described as "tongues" (Acts 2:5-12);
   b) Interpretation of aforementioned unlearned language;
   c) Prophesying (foretelling the future, not merely forth-telling already-revealed truth); and
   d) Forms of healing as used by the Apostles

It is obvious that this definition does not agree with Scripture. The Bible never presents such a case of cessation of miracles or the gifts of the Spirit.

As long as the guidelines put forth in the Word are being followed, it is up to each person to become educated in order to avoid personal confusion. If you look at the original word for confusion here, it can be seen that Paul is talking about commotion and disturbance.

Some have gone too far in order to avoid commotion by eliminated the practice of the gifts altogether. This violates what verse 39 tells us. The solution to this problem is to teach the proper way for the gifts to function.

WORD GEMS

- "Author" is added by the translators based on the context of the verse.
- "Confusion" (Gr. *akatastasia*) means "commotion, tumult, disturbance, a state of disorder."
- "Peace" (Gr. *eirene*) means "harmony, concord."

1 Corinthians 14 Section Five (34-35)

14:34 Let your women keep silent in the churches, for they are not permitted to speak; but they are to be submissive, as the law also says. 35 And if they want to learn something, let them ask their own husbands at home; for it is shameful for women to speak in church.

It appears that Paul is changing subjects here, but a closer look reveals that he is still talking about order within the worship gathering.

Paul previously gave instructions for women to both pray and prophesy in the church (chapter 11); therefore, he was not saying that women could never speak in the church. What was he saying? If you continue reading verse 35, it becomes clear that Paul was referring to asking questions. During the first century, as a carryover from the Jewish synagogue, the men would sit on one side of the church and the women on the other. It was also common for questions to be asked during the church service. Paul's instructions were for the women to keep quiet and to ask their husbands at home. Remember, this whole chapter is about protocol and order within the worship gathering.

The word "silent" in verse 34 is the same Greek word that Paul used in verse 28 about speaking in tongues without an interpreter and in verse 30 about the prophets when another has a revelation. It is clear that the silence here in verse 34 is about nothing more than order and protocol.

To carry the subject beyond the context of this passage, we may also consider Paul's instructions in **1 Timothy 2:11-12:**

> **11 Let a woman learn in silence with all submission.**
> **12 And I do not permit a woman to teach or to have authority over a man, but to be in silence.**

We see once more that the silence is in reference to learning. Further, verse 12 advises us that a woman should not teach *over* a man. The King James translates this as to "usurp authority." A woman's ministry should be under the covering of male leadership.

Consider the following partial list of women that were used by God in the Bible:

1. **Miriam** was a prophetess and one of only three spiritual leaders over the nation of Israel, along with Moses and Aaron. (Exodus 15:20)
2. **Deborah** was a judge, a prophetess and a mother of Israel for over 40 years. (Judges 4:4).
3. **Huldah** was a prophetess (2 Chron. 34:22-28).
4. **The woman of Samaria** was used by God to preach the Gospel to an entire city (John 4:39-42).

5. **Mary Magdalene** was the first to preach His resurrection (John 20:17-18). Saint Augustine wrote that she was, :The first preacher of the resurrection of Christ
6. **Philip's four daughters** were prophetesses (Acts 21:8.10).
7. **Priscilla** was a teacher and pastor along with her husband Aquila. Her ministry was received by the apostle Apollos (Acts 18:24-28).

WORD GEMS

- "Submissive" (Gr. *hypotasso*) means "to subdue, be under obedience." This is a Greek military term.
- "Shame" (Gr. *aischron*) means "dishonorable."

1 Corinthians 14 Section Six (36-40)

14:36 Or did the word of God come originally from you? Or was it you only that it reached?

This is clearly an indignant remark by Paul, their spiritual father. He asks them if they are the authors of the Word of God. The seemingly had been making up their own rules, on the fly, up to this point.

It is the responsibility of every Christian to search the Scriptures to see if what is being taught is actually according to the Word of God. The example that we find of this in Scripture are the Bereans in Acts chapter 17.

> **Acts 17:10-11**
> **10 Then the brethren immediately sent Paul and Silas away by night to Berea. When they arrived, they went into the synagogue of the Jews.**
> **11 These were more fair-minded than those in Thessalonica, in that they received the word with all readiness, and searched the Scriptures daily to find out whether these things were so.**

If you are attending church somewhere and the pastor is teaching that the gifts of the Spirit are no longer for today, get out of there and find a Bible teaching church that teaches the whole counsel of God. Conversely, If your pastor is allowing the gifts to function in a way that contradicts Paul's teaching here in chapter 14, then confront your pastor with these Scriptures. If he refuses to listen, find a church that operates within the order that God's Word sets forth.

Here in verse 36, this is also Paul's way of saying: " I have just given you divine order on how these manifestations are to be handled, will you disregard it and continue to follow your own rules, or lack thereof?"

WORD GEMS

- "Only" (Gr. *monos*) means "alone with no help."

14:37 If anyone thinks himself to be a prophet or spiritual, let him acknowledge that the things which I write to you are the commandments of the Lord.

If anyone among you sees himself as a spiritual leader, the test of validity will be his agreement with what I am writing to you. Everything that Paul has said about the proper order for these gifts is direct commandment from the Lord.

Anyone who calls himself a prophet but operates outside of the Scripture, or in contradiction to it, is not to be followed. This is clear throughout the Word of God, beginning all the way back in Deuteronomy where Moses said not to fear a prophet who speaks presumptuously (18:22). Jesus said that there would be false prophets (Matthew 24:11).

There are those who consider themselves to be so "spiritual" that they walk on a higher plane than others and receive direct revelation that is not found in the Word of God. These are counterfeit manifestations. Guard your heart from those who make these claims.

I'm aware of a man who calls himself a prophet and claims that he makes daily visits to heaven. He says that anyone can do it; just close your eyes and have faith. I categorically reject this notion. There is only one example of this in the New Testament – the apostle Paul (2 Corinthians 12). And when he shares the experience, it had been 14 years since the occurrence. As a consequence this supposed prophet's outlandish claim, I cannot receive any prophecy that he shares.

Now, when it comes to the simple exercise of prophecy, tongues and interpretation and other gifts, please note that there may be times when someone operates a gift out of compliance to these instructions, in a public meeting. Even though there may not be public correction, don't assume that there isn't correction that occurs afterwards behind the scenes. God gives leaders wisdom on how and when to administer correction and guidance.

WORD GEMS

- "Thinks himself" (Gr. *dokeo*) means "to be of the opinion or to be of the reputation."

- "Acknowledge" (Gr. *epiginosko*) means "to become thoroughly acquainted with, to know thoroughly."

14:38 But if anyone is ignorant, let him be ignorant.

After all that Paul has said, as a direct commandment from the Lord, in chapters 12 through 14, if someone chooses to be ignorant of the manifestations of the Spirit and their proper use, then let him be ignorant.

Paul starts the section of the letter by writing, "don't be ignorant" (12:1) and concludes the section by saying, "if you choose to be ignorant after all that I've taught, then remain in ignorance" (paraphrase).

Some have taken it beyond ignorance and made it their personal mission to fight against the gifts of the Spirit, especially the gift of tongues. Going so far as to say that people who practice this gift are demon possessed. There is a fine line between mocking the Holy Spirit and His gifts and blasphemy of the Holy Spirit. I would not want to put myself in that position.

Are their abuses? Of course. The Corinthians were misusing and possibly abusing these gifts. Carnality does not prevent someone from receiving a gift, just as it didn't with the Corinthians who were very carnal. Are there counterfeits? Certainly. Why would the devil bother to counterfeit something that did not also have a genuine manifestation? No one counterfeits three-dollar-bills.

The point is that the Word of God gives us clear and concise instructions for the use of these gifts. To be everything that God has called us to be, we need their operation in our midst.

WORD GEMS

- "Ignorant" (Gr. *agnoeo*) means "to not know through lack of information"

14:39 Therefore, brethren, desire earnestly to prophesy, and do not forbid to speak with tongues.

Paul tells us, "Earnestly desire to prophesy." Please note that he is not referring to the prophecy of Scripture. The Corinthians, even though living in the first century church, were not afforded the ability to give inspired Scripture. Paul's admonition is to seek to edify, exhort and comfort the church.

"Forbid not to speak with tongues." There are many excuses that the modern religious man comes up with to not allow tongues to spoken in church. One prominent radio preacher, whom I like to listen to, says the following about tongues:

> *Tongues may cause division within a church; therefore, tongues are not allowed to be expressed at meetings.*

So, because some may be offended or divided over the use of tongues, we will not allow them to be used. Is this direction found anywhere in the New Testament? The preacher, in his statement of belief, gave no scriptural support for his position to not allow tongues.

The following are some of the more prominent fallacies and the corresponding truth from God's Word.

Fallacy 1: The baptism with the Holy Spirit, with the sign of tongues is no longer for today.

This is known as the cessationist view (i.e., to come to an end). The passage of Scripture primarily used by those who adhere to this position is found in 1 Corinthians:

> **1 Corinthians 13:8-10:**
> **8 Love never fails. But whether there are prophecies, they will fail; whether there are tongues, they will cease; whether there is knowledge, it will vanish away.**
> **9 For we know in part and we prophesy in part.**
> **10 But when that which is perfect has come, then that which is in part will be done away.**

Here, Paul tells the church that there will be a time that prophecies and tongues will cease (v. 8). He goes on and explains the timing of when this will happen: *when that which is perfect is come* (v. 10). Those who hold to a cessation theology believe that this event is when the Bible was completed and no further Inspired Scripture was given. This seems logical and even believable, if only one stopped reading at verse 10. However, Paul goes on and clearly identifies the event to which he is referring.

1 Corinthians 13:11-12

11 When I was a child, I spoke as a child, I understood as a child, I thought as a child; but when I became a man, I put away childish things.

12 For now we see in a mirror, dimly, but <u>then</u> face to face. Now I know in part, but <u>then</u> I shall know just as I also am known.

The event which Paul is speaking of is when we get to Heaven! It is then that we will know just as we are known. Of course, in Heaven there is no further need for prophecies or tongues or more knowledge.

Peter, on the day of Pentecost, clarified how long and to whom the gift of the Holy Spirit was for:

Acts 2:38-39

38 Then Peter said to them, "Repent, and let every one of you be baptized in the name of Jesus Christ for the remission of sins; and you shall receive the gift of the Holy Spirit.

39 For the promise is to you and to your children, and to all who are afar off, as many as the Lord our God will call."

Fallary 2; Paul said it is better to speak five words in an understood language then to speak 10,000 words in a tongue; therefore, tongues must be of minimal value.

I want to address this on two fronts, the first of which is Paul's personal testimony. Let's read the passage in context:

> **1 Corinthians 14:18-19**
> **18 I thank my God I speak with tongues more than you all;**
> **19 yet in the church I would rather speak five words with my understanding, that I may teach others also, than ten thousand words in a tongue.**

Paul prefaces his comment about speaking in an understood language by telling the Corinthian believers that he speaks with tongues more than all of them. The literal rendering is "more than all of you put together." This certainly doesn't sound like Paul is minimizing the personal gift of tongues.

Understanding the difference between the personal use of tongues, as mentioned by Paul in verse 18, and the public gift of tongues (v. 19), helps us to arrive at the correct interpretation of what Paul is instructing.

The gift of tongues is listed in 1 Corinthians 12 as one of the nine gifts of the Spirit. This is different from the personal gift of tongues, as received through the baptism with the Holy Spirit. Faith is also listed as a gift of the Holy Spirit, but we know that there is also a personal faith that is separate from the public gift of faith. Scripture says that not everyone receives the same gifts of the Spirit for public use in the church (1 Corinthians 12:11). However, in the upper room, all 120 who were present received the baptism with the Holy Spirit and spoke in tongues – 100% of them.

What Paul is instructing in our text is that when the church comes together, it would serve no purpose to stand in front of the congregation and speak in an unknown tongue, unless there is an interpretation.   No one would be edified except the speaker.

To summarize:

Personal Use of Tongues
- Unto God
- Doesn't need interpretation
- As often as desired

Public Use of Tongues
- Before people
- Must be interpreted
- Only when the Spirit prompts

Fallacy 3: You can only pray in tongues when the Spirit moves upon you.

Paul told the Corinthians that he spoke in tongues more than all of them put together (1 Corinthians 12:18). And those people spoke in tongues – a lot! Paul knew the importance of staying connected to the power source – the Holy Spirit.

Some believers have rarely spoken in tongues since they received the initial baptism with the Holy Spirit. The baptism was not meant for a one-time experience, but a continual refreshing and empowerment.

Ephesians 5:18 And do not be drunk with wine, in which is dissipation; but be filled with the Spirit.

The literal rendering of this in the Greek is, "be being filled," as it is in the present continual tense. In other words, always be in the state of being filled. The Holy Spirit lives inside out you, but so many people are waiting for an external experience, for the Holy Spirit to **come upon** them.

Praying in tongues is a gift that must be exercised. Jude 20 tells us that this type of prayer will build us up on our most holy faith.

Fallacy 4: A believer must tarry before receiving the baptism with the Holy Spirit.

Jesus told the disciple to tarry in Jerusalem until they receive the Holy Spirit.

> **Luke 24: 49 Behold, I send the Promise of My Father upon you; but tarry in the city of Jerusalem until you are endued with power from on high.**

Up until this point, the Holy Spirit had not come. It was an unfulfilled promise until Jesus ascended to Heaven. Therefore, Jesus told them to wait.

> **John 14:16-17**
> **16 And I will pray the Father, and He will give you another Helper, that He may abide with you forever—**

17 the Spirit of truth, whom the world cannot receive, because it neither sees Him nor knows Him; but you know Him, for He dwells with you and will be in you.

Notice that Jesus said that the Father would give them the Holy Spirit, Who was currently *with* them, but in the future would be *in* them. Until Jesus ascended, the disciples only had the Holy Spirit upon them, in measure. But on the day of Pentecost, the Holy Spirit was poured out and there was no longer a need to wait or tarry for Him.

Before Pentecost
The Spirit *with* you

After Pentecost (Acts 2)
The Spirit *in* you

Fallacy 5: Speaking in tongues are a gift that not everyone can receive.

This error stems from failing to understand the distinction between the gift of speaking with different tongues (which must be interpreted) and the personal use of tongues through the indwelling Holy Spirit.

Of course, they are both gifts, but one is for public use and is only used as the Spirit wills. Not everyone receives this gift. We cover this gift more extensively in the section of the gifts of the Holy Spirit.

On the other hand, the baptism with the Holy Spirit and the accompanying sign of speaking in tongues is for every child of God. How many people were in the upper room on the day of Pentecost? How many people got filled with the Holy Spirit and began to speak in tongues? The answer to both of these questions is 120, or 100% of those present.

Listen to the promise of Jesus:

> **Luke 11:11-13**
> **11 If a son asks for bread from any father among you, will he give him a stone? Or if he asks for a fish, will he give him a serpent instead of a fish?**
> **12 Or if he asks for an egg, will he offer him a scorpion?**
> **13 If you then, being evil, know how to give good gifts to your children, how much more will your heavenly Father give the Holy Spirit to those who ask Him!"**

The baptism of the Holy Spirit is a free gift to every child of God who asks.

Fallacy 6: "If I don't understand what I am saying in tongues, I might unknowingly be cursing the Lord."

This idea is simply a manifestation of the carnal thought life trying to rationalize the things of God. We already established above, from Luke chapter 11, the following:

- If you ask the Father for a piece of bread, He won't give you a stone

- If you ask the Father for a fish, He won't give you a serpent
- If you ask the Father for an egg, He won't give you a scorpion

And most importantly, if you ask the Father for the Holy Spirit, he will not give you a counterfeit!

The Apostle Paul also addresses this concern in his first letter to the Corinthians:

> **1 Corinthians 12:3 Therefore I make known to you that no one speaking by the Spirit of God calls Jesus accursed, and no one can say that Jesus is Lord except by the Holy Spirit.**

There is absolutely no reason to fear the Holy Spirit, His presence or His baptism of power. This experience will give you power to witness for Christ.

Fallacy 7: "Tongues is a gift for the spiritually immature."

Some have reasoned that the gift of tongues is only for the spiritually immature because the Corinthians were immature and carnal. However, it must be kept in mind that Paul never told them to cease from speaking in tongues, but instead gave them teaching to do so in the correct manner.

And if speaking in tongues was for the spiritually immature, the apostle Paul must have been the most immature Christian of all, for he said in verse 19, "I thank my God I speak with tongues more than you all"

On the flip side of this question, does it mean that one cannot be spiritually mature unless he prays in tongues? I cannot say no to that question. I am aware of some great men and women of God who don't pray in tongues. However, when God makes a gift available for our benefit, it behooves us to take advantage of His kindness.

WORD GEMS

- "Forbid" (Gr. *kolyo*) means "to hinder, prevent or refuse."

14:40 Let all things be done decently and in order.

The conclusion of the matter: Let all things be done decently and in order. This does not mean that we should have dead and dry church services!

When the Holy Spirit is moving in a service, there is a peace to all that He does. However, the carnal mind of some who are present may go *Tilt! Tilt! Tilt!* On the reverse side of that, I have been in some large Spirit-filled churches (supposed) where the gifts of the Spirit were never in manifestation. Whenever we try too hard to be seeker friendly, we cut the Holy Spirit out of the process and no one is convicted and no one's life is changed.

When you have been in a church service where divine order was there and the Holy Spirit was allowed to move, it has lasting impact on your life. I have also been in some meetings, including home meetings (which should follow the same rules) that were out of control.

Balance is the key. It has been said that there are two miles of ditch for every mile of road. Some are in the ditch of the *misuse* of the gifts and others in the ditch *no use* on the other side of the road. The key is to stay in the middle of the road and do things decently and in order.

WORD GEMS

- "Decently" (Gr. *euschemonos*) means "in a seemly or honorable manner."
- "Order" (Gr. *taxis*) means "in due or right order; in the proper position or arrangement."

How to Receive the Baptism with the Holy Spirit

The following is a step-by-step guide to receiving the baptism with the Holy Spirit. By no means, do all of the steps need to be followed. However, I have included some valuable tips that I have learned over the years from helping people who struggle in this area. Sometimes the mental block is so great that one gives up and resigns to the notion that "it must not be for me." There is no need to think that way.

One may ask, "How is it that some believers have such a hard time receiving the gift of tongues today, when in the Bible people just received?" Remember, that in the early church it was fresh and new; man had not had the opportunity to complicate it yet. Now, we have had 2,000 years for man and religion to complicate and explain away this powerful gift and it sets up hindrances to some people who've been taught that the gift is not for today.

Here are some simple, basic steps for receiving:

Step One

Verse yourself in all of the promises for the Holy Spirit baptism found within the Word of God. Faith comes by hearing and hearing by the Word of God (Romans 10:17).

Tradition is a big hindrance to receiving the baptism – often Pentecostal tradition is the culprit!

Step Two

Remove from your mind any preconceived notion about how it will happen, what you will feel, and what your heavenly language will sound like. The Holy Spirit comes and manifests in different ways.

Simply trust God that He will give you the genuine and authentic gift of the Holy Spirit (Luke 11:13).

Step Three

Pray and ask the Father for the Baptism with the Holy Spirit in Jesus' name.

"Father, I ask You for the baptism with the Holy Spirit in Jesus' name, in accordance with Your Word. I am Your child, saved by the Blood of Jesus. I am hungry for more of You and desire to be empowered to serve You even greater. By faith, I receive the baptism right now."

Lift your hands to God in a surrender mode and begin to yield to the Holy Spirit.

Step Four

At this point, stop speaking in English. You cannot speak in your native language and your heavenly language at the same time.

Also, relax or open your mouth. Many people clinch their jaws shut, somehow expecting God to open their mouths for them. It does not work that way. The Holy Spirit is a Gentleman and does not force His way upon us.

Step Five

Yield your tongue to God and by faith begin to speak out whatever sound comes up. It may be a single syllable; be obedient to speak it out.

Do not allow the fear of "making it up" to rob you of God's blessing. The Father will NOT give you a counterfeit!

Keep speaking! Sometimes the faucet starts with a drip and a drop, but there's more coming!

Step Six

Purpose to pray to God in tongues every day. Do not allow your gift to become stagnant. Ephesians 5:18 literally says, "Be being filled with the Spirit." This means, continually exercise your gift.

Do not wait for the Holy Spirit to "come upon you" and "inspire" you to pray in tongues. This is the reason that some Christians rarely speak in tongues. They have confused the public gift of tongues with the personal gift of tongues. The Holy Spirit dwells in you now. Refer to all of the benefits of praying in tongues in the section, "Why Every Believer Should Pray in Tongues."

1 Corinthians 14:32-33 says, *And the spirits of the prophets are subject to the prophets. For God is not the author of confusion but of peace, as in all the churches of the saints.* This means that you are in control of the gift; you use it as often or as seldom as you want and as loud or as soft as you want.

Some Pentecostals believe that you must quiver and shake when speaking in tongues... that there must be accompanying physical and/or emotional displays. That's fine if they choose to do that (as long as it's not disruptive), but it is not necessary in any way.

In closing, as believers living in the end-times, we have been given a tremendous opportunity to impact our world for Christ. The church needs all of the spiritual weapons that the Holy Spirit has given to the body.

Pursue love and desire spiritual gifts!

Other books by David Chapman

Blood Covenant

The Believer's Deliverance Handbook

The Fullness of the Spirit

Modern Day Apostles

The Pattern and the Glory

Made in the USA
Middletown, DE
24 February 2023

25319329R00046